THE UNIVERSE

The Outer Planets

Revised and Updated

Tim Goss and Geza Gyuk

www.heinemann.co.uk/library

Visit our website to find out more information about Heinemann Library books.

To order:

☎ Phone 44 (0) 1865 888066

📄 Send a fax to 44 (0) 1865 314091

🖥 Visit the Heinemann Bookshop at www.heinemann.co.uk/library to browse our catalogue and order online.

First published in Great Britain by Heinemann, Halley Court, Jordan Hill, Oxford, OX2 8EJ, part of Harcourt Education.
Raintree is a registered trademark of Harcourt Education Ltd.

Editorial: Nick Hunter and Rachel Howells
Design: Richard Parker and Tinstar Design
Illustrations: Calvin J. Hamilton
Picture Research: Mica Brancic
Production: Julie Carter

Originated by Modern Age
Printed and bound in China by Leo Paper Group

ISBN 978 0 4311 5476 3
11 10 09 08 07
10 9 8 7 6 5 4 3 2 1

British Library Cataloguing in Publication Data
Goss, Tim, 1958-
The outer planets. - (The universe)
523.4
A full catalogue record for this book is available from the British Library.

Acknowledgements
The Publishers would like to thank the following for permission to reproduce photographs: The author and publisher are grateful to the following for permission to reproduce copyright material: p. 4 NASA/Ames Research Center/Rick Guidice; pp. 5, 11 Science Photo Library, p. 23 Alan Stern/Southwest Research Institute, Marc Buie/Lowell Observatory, NASA and ESA; p. 6 D. Van Ravenswaay/Photo Researchers, Inc.; pp. 7, 10 Bettman/Corbis; p. 8 Hulton-Deutsch Collection/Corbis; p. 9 Mary Evans Picture Library; pp. 11, 24, 25 Courtesy of Calvin J. Hamilton/www.solarviews.com; pp. 12, 13, 15R, 16, 18, 20, 21, 26, 28, 29 NASA/JPL/Caltech; p. 14 Dr. R. Albrecht, ESA/ESO Space Telescope European Coordinating Facility, and NASA; p. 15L Kenneth Seidelmann/U.S. Naval Observatory and NASA; p. 17 Science Photo Library/NASA / ESA / STSCI / E.Karkoschka, U.Arizona; p. 19 Erich Karkoschka/University of Arizona Lunar & Planetary Lab and NASA; p. 22 H. Hammel/Massachusetts Institute of Technology and NASA; p. 27 Eliot Young/Southwest Research Institute et al., and NASA

Cover photograph: Science Photo Library/Detlev Van Ravenswaay

The publishers would like to thank Geza Gyuk of the Adler Planetarium, Chicago, for his assistance in the preparation of this book.

Every effort has been made to contact copyright holders of any material reproduced in this book. Any omissions will be rectified in subsequent printings if notice is given to the publishers.

Contents

Any words appearing in the text in bold, **like this**, are explained in the Glossary.

Which are the outer planets?

Uranus and Neptune are the outer **planets:** the seventh and eighth in our **solar system**. They were the first new planets to be discovered since ancient times. After Uranus was discovered people were very excited that there might be more planets. For a while even some of the large **asteroids** were considered planets. The discovery of Neptune made people even more excited.

Pluto is ninth in the solar system. When Pluto was discovered in 1930 **astronomers** immediately called it a planet. Today, astronomers do not think that Pluto is a planet like Uranus and Neptune. In fact, Pluto is very different from all of the first eight planets.

Why is Pluto's orbit different?

The **orbits** of Uranus and Neptune are almost perfect circles, similar to the orbits of the inner planets like Earth. Pluto's orbit looks like a long, stretched-out circle. At one point in its orbit, Pluto crosses Neptune's orbit. At that point, Pluto is closer to the Sun than Neptune is. Pluto's orbit is also tilted unlike the planets.

The outer planets are the ones furthest from the Sun, at the bottom of this picture.

This is a computer artwork of three of the dwarf planets in the solar system. Eris is shown on the left, Pluto is in the middle, and Ceres is on the right.

Pluto is very small

Pluto is much smaller than astronomers first thought. Instead of being about the size of Earth, Pluto has a mass almost 30 times smaller than even tiny Mercury, the smallest planet in our solar system.

Pluto is not alone

The eight planets close to the Sun all orbit alone. Pluto seems to be only one of billions of similar very cold icy objects. These objects make up the Kuiper Belt. This is where many **comets** come from.

Most of the Kuiper Belt objects are very small, but in 2005 astronomers discovered Eris, which is a bit bigger than Pluto. We know at least ten other objects that are nearly as large as Pluto. There may be hundreds of Kuiper Belt objects as large as or larger than Pluto.

Dwarf planets

Because of all these differences, in 2006 astronomers voted to re-classify Pluto and Eris as **dwarf planets**. Pluto is not considered a full planet anymore, but it is still very interesting to astronomers. Pluto was the first member of the Kuiper Belt discovered and we know the most about it. Learning about Pluto tells us what the Kuiper Belt objects and other dwarf planets are like.

Where in the sky are the outer planets?

On a clear night, you might be able to see Uranus with **binoculars**. It is almost 2,700 million kilometres (1,700 million miles) from Earth. Neptune is about 4,300 million kilometres (2,700 million miles) from Earth. You can only see it with a **telescope**. Pluto is usually more than 5,500 million kilometres (3,500 million miles) from Earth. Eris is even further, usually more than 10,000 million kilometres (6,000 million miles) away. You cannot see either Pluto or Eris very well from Earth, even with a telescope.

The solar system

The **solar system** is made of all the **planets**, **moons**, **comets**, and **asteroids** that circle the Sun. The Sun's **gravity** pulls on all of the objects in our solar system. If it were not for the pull of the Sun, the planets would travel in straight lines. This would send them out into deep space! The force of gravity keeps the planets in regular paths around the Sun called **orbits**.

The outer planets have further to go in their orbits around the Sun. They have to make a larger circle because they are so far away.

Years and years and years

Earth's orbit around the Sun takes about 365 **days**. We call that time period one Earth **year**. Uranus needs about 84 Earth years to complete one orbit. Neptune needs 164 Earth years to complete one orbit. It takes Pluto about 248 Earth years to orbit the Sun.

Why is it so hard to find the outer planets?

Uranus, Neptune, and the **dwarf planets** are so far away from the Sun that very little sunlight reaches them. The small amount of sunlight the planets **reflect** is not enough for them to be easily visible from Earth.

Think of what it is like to sit by a campfire. The people closest to the fire get the most warmth from it. In the same way, the planets closest to the Sun get more light and heat from it than the ones that are further away. It is easiest for people on Earth to see the planets that are reflecting the most sunlight.

The best views of Pluto have come from the Hubble Space Telescope.

How were the outer planets discovered?

An **astronomer** called William Herschel found Uranus in 1781. He had been searching the night skies with his **telescope** to study **stars**. At first, Herschel thought Uranus was a **comet** or star. Earlier astronomers who had seen it thought it was another star. In 1690, one astronomer even named this "new star". However, Herschel observed that it did not have a tail like a comet. It also moved slowly, showing that it must be in **orbit**. This meant that it had to be a **planet**, not a star.

William Herschel and others had noticed that the orbit of Uranus was different from what they had expected. Uranus moved as if forces from beyond the Sun and the other planets were tugging at it. This suggested that another planet was there. This was found to be Neptune.

How was Neptune discovered?

No one had ever seen Neptune before it was discovered in 1846. One reason is that it cannot be seen without a telescope. The other reason is that until Uranus was discovered, **astronomers**

William Herschel was born in Germany but was living in England when he discovered the planet Uranus. His sister Caroline took notes on his findings.

thought that the first six planets were the whole **solar system**. No one had even looked for more planets.

In 1846 two mathematicians, John Couch Adams in England and Urbain-Jean-Joseph Le Verrier in France, began to use mathematical formulas to work out the position of another planet that could be affecting Uranus's orbit.

Both mathematicians sent their predictions of where there might be another planet to astronomers. When the astronomers looked where the mathematicians had predicted they saw a new star that moved. They knew they had discovered a new planet.

How were the planets named?

Uranus was named after the Greek god of the heavens. The god Uranus was the father of Saturn and the grandfather of Jupiter. Neptune is named for the Roman god of the sea.

John Couch Adams (1819–92) was one of the people who discovered the planet Neptune.

How were the dwarf planets discovered?

Astronomers had thought there might be a **planet** beyond Uranus because of the path of Uranus's **orbit**. Soon the pattern of Neptune's movements led scientists to think there was yet another planet beyond it. In the early 1900s, an American astronomer, Percival Lowell, led the search for this planet from an **observatory** in Arizona. Lowell died in 1916, but an **amateur** astronomer, Clyde Tombaugh, continued the search.

Tombaugh took photographs of the sky and compared them from night to night. On 18 February 1930, Tombaugh found something in the photos that looked like a very dim **star**. However, it was moving very slowly, and stars do not move. Tombaugh had discovered Pluto.

After Tombaugh discovered Pluto astronomers soon realized that it was much too small to change Neptune's orbit. Later astronomers realized their measurements of Neptune's orbit had been wrong.

The moving "star" that Clyde Tombaugh located was actually Pluto.

This is an artwork of the dwarf planet Eris and its moon Dysnomia. At first Eris was nicknamed Xena by its discoverers, and Dysnomia was nicknamed Gabrielle.

For many years after Pluto was discovered no other objects were found on the edge of the **solar system**. Pluto was considered a planet even though it was very small and had a strange oval orbit more like a **comet** than a planet.

By the end of the 1900s astronomers began to think that there must be many large objects beyond the orbit of Neptune. Astronomers call anything beyond Neptune a Trans-Neptunian Object or TNO. Pluto was the first TNO discovered.

In 1992 the object "1992 QB1" was discovered. It is almost a quarter of the size of Pluto. As **telescopes** improved after 1990, searches for TNOs kept finding larger and larger objects beyond Neptune. Finally, Eris, an object larger than Pluto, was discovered in 2005.

Astronomers have realized that Pluto is only the brightest, but not the largest TNO. In 2006 astronomers voted to call the largest TNOs, Pluto and Eris, **dwarf planets**. There may be many more, maybe tens or hundreds of dwarf planets.

Are all the outer planets the same?

Uranus and Neptune are both **gas** giants. They share many similarities but they are also different in many ways. Pluto and the **dwarf planets** are very different from Uranus and Neptune.

One **day** is the time it takes for a planet to spin once on its **axis**. On Earth, one day is 24 hours long. The length of a day on Uranus or Neptune is much shorter. A Uranus day is about 17 hours long, and Neptune's day is about 16 hours.

Pluto spins very slowly and its day is much longer than an Earth day. One day on Pluto is about as long as six and one-third Earth days. That is almost one week on Earth. No one knows how long it takes for Eris to spin once. It is just too far away for **astronomers** to know for certain.

Mercury
0.1°

Venus
177°

Earth
23°

Mars
25°

Jupiter
3°

Saturn
27°

Uranus
98°

Neptune
30°

Pluto
120°

Scientists think that Uranus and Pluto might have been knocked into their tilted positions by large **meteors** long ago.

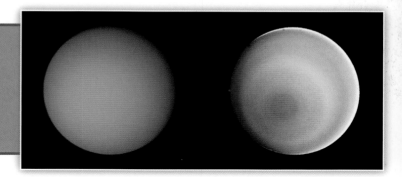

Uranus and Pluto are tipped over

Each planet is tilted on its axis. This means that the planet leans to one side. Most planets just lean a little. The tilt of Earth as it moves around the Sun causes the seasons. Neptune's tilt is almost the same as Earth's. Uranus leans so much that the planet is on its side. Instead of the north pole being at the top of the planet and the south pole being at the bottom, Uranus's **equator** runs from top to bottom. Pluto tilts even more than Uranus.

Many planets, many colours

Uranus and Neptune are two of the four planets known as the gas giants. The other two are Jupiter and Saturn. The way the **methane** gas in their **atmospheres** is affected by light makes both Uranus and Neptune look blue. Light from the Sun is made of waves of different colours. You can see these colours when there is a rainbow in the sky. When the Sun shines on Uranus and Neptune, the methane soaks up the red parts of the light. The light that is left is **reflected** back into space. The light that is left looks blue.

Pluto and Eris are not gas planets. They have a solid surface covered with ice. Some photos show that Pluto is reddish brown. Parts of Pluto look whitish, perhaps from frost. Eris reflects nearly all the light that falls on it. It seems to be covered in pure white methane "snow". Other large TNOs are different colours, from grey to red.

How big are the outer planets?

Uranus is the third largest **planet** in our **solar system**. Only Saturn and Jupiter are larger. If Uranus was empty, about 61 Earths could fit inside it. Neptune is also much bigger than Earth. About 58 Earths could fit inside Neptune. The **dwarf planets**, Pluto and Eris, are much smaller. They are so small that you could put over 150 of them inside an empty Earth.

Uranus and Neptune have lots of moons

Uranus has at least 27 **moons**. William Herschel discovered the two largest, Titania and Oberon, in 1787. Ten moons were found by the *Voyager 2* **space probe** in 1986. More are being discovered. Four were found in 2003 and there could be more. Uranus's moon Miranda is very strange. It has more **craters**, canyons, and high cliffs than other moons. Scientists think it may have been an object that was broken apart at one time. Then the pieces came back together to form a new moon.

Neptune has at least 13 moons. Six moons were discovered by *Voyager 2* in 1989. The largest moon is Triton. It was found in 1846, about two weeks after the **planet** was discovered.

Oberon, Uranus's outermost moon, has an icy surface covered with craters.

Pluto and its moon Charon are so close that photographs usually show only one object. Only photographs taken from the Hubble Space **Telescope** or using special equipment clearly show Pluto and Charon as separate objects.

Most moons **orbit** their planets in the same direction as the planet turns on its **axis**. Triton orbits Neptune in the opposite direction. It is one of just two moons in our solar system that do this. Phoebe, one of Saturn's moons, is the other. Triton is also the coldest place in the solar system ever visited by a spacecraft. The temperature on Triton's surface is about -235°C (-391°F). Pluto and Eris are even colder during most of their orbits around the Sun.

Pluto and Eris have moons

Pluto has three moons: Charon, Nix, and Hydra. Nix and Hydra are very small, but Charon is almost half the size of Pluto. Its orbit is very close to Pluto. If you were standing on the surface of Pluto, Charon would look almost seven times larger than the Moon does from Earth. Eris has one moon, Dysnomia.

How's the weather on the outer planets?

Uranus's seasons are more than 20 Earth **years** long. This is because the **planet** is tilted on its side during its 84-year **orbit** around the **Sun**. As Uranus **revolves**, the Sun shines on one pole for about 20 years. During this time, the other half of the planet is in darkness. Then, the Sun shines on the **equator** for the same period of time. Next, it shines on the other pole and, finally, the other side of the equator.

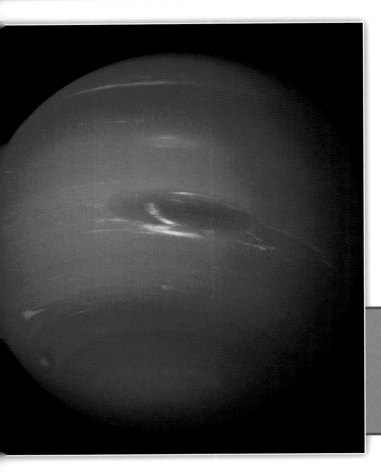

Uranus has a very thick **atmosphere**, which gives off heat from the Sun. Because of this there is not much difference in temperature between the sunny and dark parts. Near the top of the clouds, the average temperature is about -210°C (-346°F).

On Neptune, not even the parts that are tilted towards the Sun get warm.

Neptune's **axis** is tilted almost like Earth's. However, it is so far from the Sun that it does not have seasons. The round orbit means that the planet is almost always the same distance from the Sun. Neptune's temperature at the top of the clouds is about -220°C (-364°F).

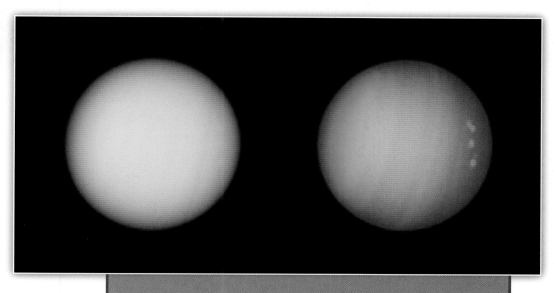

These are Hubble Space Telescope images of Uranus. The image on the left shows the planet's true colour. The image on the right has been taken using filters to bring out the detail in the cloud bands.

Pluto and Eris

Even though no **space probe** has ever visited these **dwarf planets**, **satellites** and the Hubble Space **Telescope** have given us some information. Pluto surface temperature seems to be between -230°C (-400°F) and -220°C (-360°F). Eris gets even colder than that! The orbits of Pluto and Eris are very long stretched-out circles called ovals. When they are at the far end of their orbits, very far away from the Sun, it gets much colder.

Is there air on the outer planets?

We think of air as a **gas** that we can breathe. On Earth, the air we breathe is a mixture of **nitrogen** and **oxygen**. Of the two gases, oxygen is the one we need to breathe. The outer **planets** also have a mix of gases in their **atmospheres**. However, humans cannot breathe this air because there is no oxygen.

The atmospheres of Uranus and Neptune

The atmospheres of Uranus and Neptune are made up mostly of **hydrogen** and **helium** gas. Uranus and Neptune also have a small amount of water and **methane** gas in their upper atmospheres. Uranus has a tiny bit of **ammonia** in its atmosphere. Uranus's clouds are the brightest of all the outer planets.

Scientists think that the atmospheres of Uranus and Neptune have three main layers of clouds below the outer methane cloud layer.

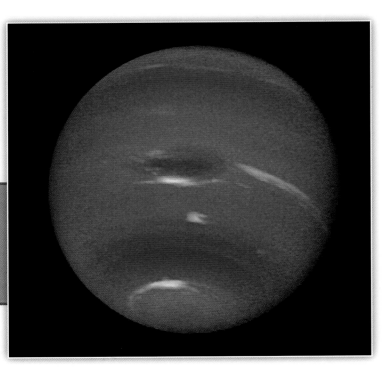

Neptune's blue-green atmosphere has clouds scattered throughout.

Colour filters were used in this image to show the layers of Uranus's atmosphere.

The top layer is made of ammonia clouds. The middle cloud layer is made from ammonia and **sulphur**. The bottom cloud layer of each planet is probably made of frozen water.

Frozen atmospheres

Pluto is so cold that its atmosphere may only be in a gas state when the planet is closest to the Sun. When Pluto is further from the Sun, the gases probably freeze into ice, leaving Pluto without an atmosphere. Eris is even further from the Sun and colder. It probably never has an atmosphere. Some scientists think maybe it has a thin atmosphere for a few years when it is at its very closest to the Sun. They think this might be where the methane snow that makes Eris so white comes from.

Cloud streaks in Neptune's atmosphere range from 50 to 200 kilometres (31 to 124 miles) across.

Scientists did not know for sure that Pluto had an **atmosphere** until 1988. **Astronomers** on Earth watched Pluto move in front of a **star**. Before the star disappeared behind the **planet**, it looked less bright. The **gases** in Pluto's atmosphere covered the star before the planet did. It was like looking at a bright light through a smoky haze. The thin atmosphere is mostly made of **nitrogen** gas with much smaller amounts of the gases **methane** and **carbon monoxide**.

Windy weather

Based on the information scientists have so far, Uranus seems to have fewer storms than any of the gas giant planets. The storms it does have, however, involve high wind speeds. In 1999, pictures from the Hubble Space **Telescope** showed storm patterns on Uranus moving the clouds at more than 500 kilometres (300 miles) per hour.

Neptune has the fastest winds of any planet. In 1989, *Voyager 2* found a storm system that scientists called the Great Dark Spot. It was as big as Earth and moved at about 1,200 kilometres (745 miles) per hour. The Great Dark Spot later disappeared, but another large spot was found in 1997. *Voyager 2* also found a small, fast-moving cloud that blows around the planet every 16 hours. Scientists studying it have called it the Scooter.

One reason for Neptune's fast winds may be that it gives off more heat than it gets from the Sun. This heat warms the air as it escapes. The warm air rises and pushes around the colder air, creating winds.

We will have to wait for a **space probe** to learn more about the winds of Pluto and Eris. So far, scientists think that even if these **dwarf planets** have a thin atmosphere it is very calm.

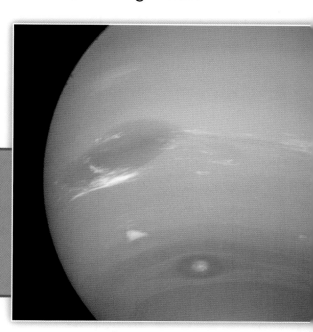

Neptune's most recognizable features are the Great Dark Spot, the Scooter (just below the Great Dark Spot), and what is known as Dark Spot 2 (further down).

What would I see if I went to the outer planets?

Uranus and Neptune are **gas** giants and do not have solid surfaces. The **atmosphere** of Uranus gets thicker and thicker until it becomes a partly liquid "icy" material. The liquid is made of water, **methane**, and **ammonia**. If you had a spaceship that could explore oceans as well as outer space, you would see that the liquid material extends deep into the **planet**. Neptune has an ocean similar to the one on Uranus.

Bring your ice skates to the dwarf planets

Pluto and Eris's surfaces are covered with ice made of frozen methane, frozen **carbon monoxide**, and some **nitrogen**. When Pluto and Eris are far from the Sun all the gases are frozen and fall as snow. When Pluto is closer to the Sun, those parts of the atmosphere become gas again. The methane ice **reflects** a lot of light and makes Pluto and Eris look bright. The Hubble Space **Telescope** has shown that Pluto has **polar caps** at the top and bottom parts of the planet. Eris seems to be bright over all of its surface.

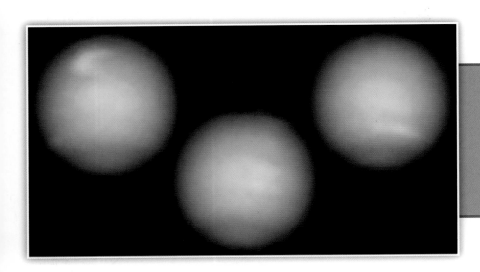

These three images of Neptune show the movement of the planet's clouds.

How can ice be hot?

For a scientist, "icy" does not always refer to what we think of as ice. The term can also be used to describe the composition of a material, or the general qualities of something. The ice on Pluto or Triton can be made of frozen carbon dioxide (what we call "dry ice"), water, methane, or ammonia. The "icy" oceans on Uranus and Neptune are also not frozen water. They are actually very hot.

Polar caps are huge pieces of ice that form on the top and bottom parts of a planet where it does not get much sunlight. The Hubble Space Telescope also found dark spots near Pluto's **equator**. Scientists are not sure yet what the spots are.

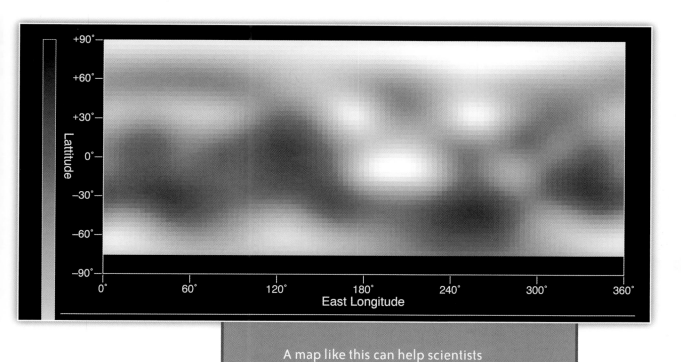

A map like this can help scientists study the bright and dark points on the surface of Pluto.

What's inside the outer planets?

Some **planets**, such as Earth and Mars, have clear lines between their **atmosphere**, **crust**, **mantle**, and **core**. With the **gas** giants like Uranus and Neptune, there is not a clear line between the atmosphere and the rest of the planet. It is more of a gradual change. Pluto and Eris are not gas giants, and do have separate layers inside.

Uranus and Neptune are liquid on the inside

In the thicker, deeper part of the atmosphere of Uranus and Neptune, each planet is made of materials that are a partly liquid "ice". This is what we call the ocean on these planets. Beneath the ocean-like atmosphere, the cores of the planets are rocky.

How is Uranus different from the other gas giants?

When the planets first formed long ago, all their inside parts were very hot. Over time, each planet slowly cooled down. The heat in their cores flowed to the outside of the planet. That is still happening to three of the gas giant planets. But Uranus is different from the other planets because its core does not give off very much heat. Scientists do not yet know why Uranus is different in this way.

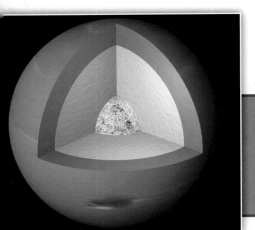

Neptune does not actually have clearly defined layers like this diagram. They blend into one another. This diagram helps give us a general idea of where changes take place.

What is inside the dwarf planets?

Scientists know very little about the **dwarf planets** because they are so far away from Earth. We know the most about Pluto. Under Pluto's icy surface and crust, there may be a mantle of water ice. Under that, the planet may have a rocky core. Scientists believe that Pluto's rocky core makes up over half of the planet.

Uranus does not have clearly defined layers either. The atmosphere changes gradually, as it does on Neptune.

Could I ever go to the outer planets?

Are you sure you want to go? The **space probe** *Voyager 2* took almost eight and a half years to get to Uranus. That includes the time it spent visiting Jupiter and Saturn along the way. After leaving Uranus, *Voyager 2* needed three and a half more years to get to Neptune. No space probe has been to Pluto or Eris. Even if there was a spacecraft that could support people on the long voyage to the outer **planets**, there would still be problems to worry about.

Imagine that you needed to talk to the people at the space centre on Earth right away. It would take more than five hours for your message to reach them if you were close to Neptune. Then it would take just as long for their answer to get back to you.

Voyager 2 took one of the first images of Neptune's rings.

Visiting Uranus and Neptune with Voyager 2

Even though visits by people to the outer planets are not possible at this time, we have still been able to learn a lot about Uranus and Neptune. The *Voyager 2* space probe found ten new **moons** and two more rings around Uranus. It also found six more moons and three more rings around Neptune.

Pluto will finally get a visitor

The National Aeronautics and Space Administration (NASA) has sent a space mission to Pluto. The *New Horizons* mission was launched in January 2006. It will fly by Pluto and its moons Charon, Nix, and Hydra in 2015. Scientists hope to learn about Pluto's moons, **atmosphere**, surface, and interior during this mission. Beyond Pluto, *New Horizons* will visit other Kuiper Belt objects even further from the Sun. No one knows how far space travel will take us.

This image shows Pluto's true colour. The image looks blurry because it is made up of many smaller images put together. Scientists have a hard time getting clear images of Pluto because it is so far away from Earth.

Fact File

Average distance from the Sun

EARTH	150 million kilometres (93 million miles)
URANUS	2.9 billion kilometres (1.8 billion miles)
NEPTUNE	4.5 billion kilometres (2.8 billion miles)
PLUTO	6 billion kilometres (3.7 billion miles)
ERIS	10.1 billion kilometres (6 billion miles)

Length of a year

EARTH	1 Earth **year**
URANUS	84 Earth years
NEPTUNE	164 Earth years
PLUTO	248 Earth years
ERIS	557 Earth years

Diameter at the equator

EARTH	12,756 kilometres (7,926 miles)
URANUS	51,118 kilometres (31,770 miles)
NEPTUNE	49,572 kilometres (30,809 miles)
PLUTO	2,300 kilometres (1,430 miles)
ERIS	2,400 kilometres (1,500 miles)

Triton is one of Neptune's **moons**. It is about the same size as Pluto and Eris. It is probably a captured Kuiper Belt object similar to Pluto and Eris.

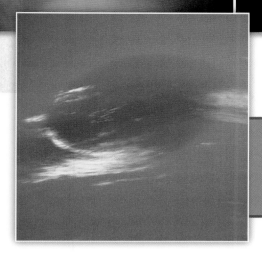

Neptune's spiral-shaped Great Dark Spot is probably a storm that rotates anticlockwise.

Length of one day

EARTH	24 hours
URANUS	17 hours
NEPTUNE	16 hours
PLUTO	6 1/3 Earth **days**
ERIS	unknown

Atmosphere

EARTH	**nitrogen, oxygen**
URANUS	**hydrogen, helium**, and **methane gas**
NEPTUNE	hydrogen, helium, and methane gas
PLUTO	very thin nitrogen and methane
ERIS	probably none

Number of moons and rings

EARTH	1 moon and no rings
URANUS	27 moons and 11 rings
NEPTUNE	13 moons and 5 rings
PLUTO	3 moons and no rings
ERIS	1 moon and no rings

Temperature range

EARTH'S SURFACE	-69°C to 58°C (-92°F to 136°F)
URANUS	-210°C (-346°F) to ??? (increases with depth)
NEPTUNE	-220°C (-364°F) to ??? (increases with depth)
PLUTO	-240 to -218°C (-400 to -360°F)
ERIS	-250 to -230°C (-418 to -382°F)

Glossary

amateur someone who does something as a hobby that other people do as a career

ammonia strong-smelling gas found in the atmospheres of many planets

asteroid large piece of floating rock that formed at the same time as the planets

astronomer person who studies objects in outer space

atmosphere all of the gases that surround an object in outer space

axis imaginary line through the middle of an object in space, around which it rotates

binoculars handheld equipment used for seeing far-away things more closely

carbon monoxide gas made up of a mixture of carbon and oxygen

comet ball of ice and rock that orbits around the Sun

core material at the centre of a planet

crater bowl-shaped hole in the ground that is made by a meteorite crashing into it

crust top, solid layer of an object in outer space. The outer part of the crust is called the surface.

day time it takes for a planet to spin on its axis once

dwarf planet planet that is too small to be considered a full planet. Pluto and Eris have been re-classified as dwarf planets.

equator imaginary line around the middle of a planet

gas substance that makes up a planet's atmosphere

gravity invisible force that pulls an object towards the centre of another object in space

helium gas found on many planets; used on Earth to make balloons float in the air

hydrogen substance found on many planets

mantle middle layer of a planet or moon. It lies between the core and the crust.

meteor piece of rock or dust that travels in outer space

methane gas found in the atmosphere of some planets in our solar system

moon object that floats in an orbit around a planet

nitrogen gas found in the atmosphere of Earth and some of the other planets in our solar system

observatory place with high-powered telescopes where astronomers study the stars and planets

orbit curved path of one object in space moving around another object; or, to take such a path under the influence of gravity

oxygen gas that is found in the atmosphere of Earth. Humans and animals breathe it in.

planet large object in space that orbits a central star and does not produce its own light

polar cap large piece of ice that covers the north or south pole of a planet and does not receive much sunlight

reflect bounce back

revolve when a planet travels around the Sun, or when a moon travels around a planet

satellite shortened version of the term artificial satellite, meaning a machine made to orbit Earth

solar system group of objects in space that all float in orbits around a central star

space probe ship that carries computers and other instruments to study objects in outer space

star glowing ball of gases in outer space that produces light and energy through a process of nuclear reactions

sulphur yellow-coloured powdery material; found on many planets in gas form

telescope instrument used by astronomers to study objects in outer space

year time it takes for a planet to complete one orbit around the Sun

More books to read

Neptune, Gregory L. Vogt (Capstone, 2006)

Uranus, Thomas K. Adamson (Capstone, 2006)

Why Isn't Pluto a Planet?: A Book about Planets, Stephen J. Kortenkamp (Capstone, 2007)

Index